Cats

CATS

Cats
in the
Animal World

The lynx is one of the most solitary, reclusive cats in the northern hemisphere. It vies with the wolf for the status of great predator in the snowy forests.

Wild cats and their cousins

All cats, whether wild or domesticated, belong to the elegant feline race. The cat family is extensive, and each of its members, from the smallest to the largest – the Siberian tiger – is essentially an elite hunter, designed to stalk its prey for hours, pounce on it and kill it in one bite.

The tiger is the largest of the domestic cat's relatives. Like the cat, the tiger is a fearsome hunter whose patience is only matched by its impressive speed of action.

The domestic cat belongs to the large family of Felidae, a group which encompasses all species of cats. From the majestic panther to the ordinary alley cat, all members of the feline race share several common features: all are carnivores, and they all have round heads and short faces. Their formidable claws make them fearsome hunters, and they can spy on their prey for several hours, keeping perfectly still, before pouncing on it. Cats are renowned for their

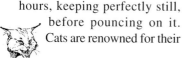

Lying in wait for its prey, the tiger is a big cat who is a master of the art of camouflage.

With its thick fur, the lynx can tolerate snow and copes with the harshest of climates without difficulty.

The panther, also called the leopard, is a feline whose behaviour and attitudes are reminiscent of the domestic cat. Independent by nature, the panther leads a solitary life.

grace, nonchalance, and agility. All cats have this much in common, but they can be differentiated by certain distinctive traits: only lions are capable of roaring because of the unique morphology of their jaws, tigers and panthers can growl, whereas the rest – the smallest – can only miaow.

Three feline groups

The Felidae family consists of three genuses. The Panthera genus includes all species of

Even if the puma is the size of a panther, this big American cat purrs.

felines that can be classed as 'big cats': the lion, the tiger, the leopard (or panther), and the jaguar. The cheetah, the only member of the Acinonyx genus, is a champion sprinter with non-retractable claws that ensure perfect 'road-holding' at high speed. The third category of felines is the Felis genus which includes all other cats.

Close cousins

The cats belonging to the Felis genus are average or small in size. The lynx is the only member of the genus that will not eat carrion. The Felis genus also includes the ocelot, found in mainland America, whose beautifully marked coat has been highly sought after. The serval, a good swimmer and an expert fisher, lives near watercourses in Africa. The Jungle cat, most common in South-East Asia, is one of the largest cats in the genus weighing about 20 kilograms – around twice the weight of its cousins. The largest member of Felis, the American puma (or cougar), is almost as big as a leopard. Finally, there are a number of species of wildcat which live in habitats ranging

The cheetah is the fastest land mammal in the world.

Despite its impressive size - up to 3.5 metres from the tip of its nose to the end of its tail and weighing up to 250 kilograms - the tiger is an animal of amazing agility.

▼ The panther, or leopard, which once lived all over the world, is only found today in Africa and Asia. Males can weigh up to 90 kilograms, and females up to 60 kilograms. Its soft coat can be black but is usually spotted, giving it a very efficient camouflage in its hunting ground. The leopard can haul a carcass much bigger than itself up a tree, a favourite place of refuge. Its graceful movement and its overall morphology make it one of the wild cats most closely related to the domestic cat.

Little is known about the reclusive jaguarundi. This strange wild cat is found in the forests of Central America.

from deserts to northern forests.

Surviving ancestors

Two species of wild cats are precursors of the domestic cat: the African wildcat (*Felis sylvestris libyca*), which lives in the Sahara desert, and the European wildcat (*Felis sylvestris europeus*), which has almost disappeared from the forests of Europe. This timid animal was progressively exterminated because of the havoc it caused in

The wildcat of Europe's forests is a secretive feline and an excellent hunter.

henhouses. Zoologists were quick to classify the European wildcat as the ancestor the domestic cat, because of physical similarities. However, a recent study of mummified Egyptian cats from the first century BC confirmed that the modern domestic cat is descended from the African wildcat. This hypothesis is reinforced by the etymology of the word 'cat', which comes from the Arabic word 'qattah'. But whether it is of European or African origin, the elegant

The African wildcat is a very close relative of today's domestic cat.

The serval, characterized by its long legs and large, erect ears, is a born hunter that lives a nomadic existence in the African savannah.

The jaguar is the panther of South America. The king of the Amazonian forest, it will attack any prey that crosses its territory, including tortoises and caymans.

Living in the Pliocene era (the era of large mammals, between seven and two million years ago), sabre-toothed tigers used their enormous canines like daggers. They were not afraid to attack huge beasts such as the slow-moving, thick-skinned mammoths. With climatic warming and the progressive extinction of large herbivores, these giant cats proved incapable of hunting smaller, and crucially, more agile prey.

Lions, unlike domestic cats, live in organized social groups.

creature purring by the fireside and sharing its life with humans has a much longer history.

The cat's prehistory

About 35 to 40 million years ago an animal the size of a weasel existed called the miacis. This little carnivore is the ancestor of many carnivorous species, such as the wolf, the bear, the hyena and the racoon, as well as all the cats, whether large or small. Several tens of millions of years later, this species diversified producing dinictis, the true great-grandparent of Felidae. This animal, living in the Miocene era, is also the oldest member of an extinct family of sabre-toothed tiger-cats that includes the smilodon. These fearsome prehistoric predators armed with sharp canines but with a poorly developed brain became extinct at the same time as their favourite prey, the mammoth. Sabre-toothed tigers have no surviving descendant. Panthers, which at the time were found all around the world, fared better. Wildcats in their present form appeared around one and a half million years ago, whereas the first known domestic cat dates back to ancient Egypt.

For all the nobility of its race, the domestic cat is a relentless adventurer who loves to climb trees to flush birds out from their nests.

The domestic cat's lifestyle

Whether living in the country or in towns, the small feline has kept its predator's instincts in its morphology and its temperament. Yet this incredible hunting machine can enjoy lazy moments, and from a very young age it loves playing.

Cats are well adapted to city life, where they recreate a world in which they can express all of their instincts.

The cat's movements always give an impression of grace, ease, and even nonchalance. Its incredible natural litheness allows it to take the kinds of risks that would make the most gifted contortionist green with envy. But the cat's apparent laziness hides its ability to shake off its lethargy instantaneously and set a powerful mechanism in motion for sudden pouncing, climbing, jumping, scratching or biting. Its body seems so flexible as to appear

The cat enjoys dominant positions, and is inquisitive about everything.

An unrivalled tightrope walker, the cat is self-confident and can give absolute concentration to its intended victim without having to concern itself with support.

All cats practise a style of hunting based on stalking. Remaining perfectly still, the little feline springs its attack in an unpredictable way.

boneless. Indeed, the domestic cat's extraordinary anatomy is a true masterpiece of nature.

The cat's skeleton and muscles

A cat's body, like that of a leopard or a lion, is designed for hunting. Its skeleton, with the spinal column at the top, is particularly flexible. Furthermore, the cat's shoulder is detached from the main skeleton, enabling it to turn its legs in any direction

With its legendary suppleness, the cat can adopt incredible postures.

As the cat rarely suffers from vertigo, it is capable of scaling dangerous heights without suffering any anxiety.

▼ The cat's perfect physical proportions, its extremely supple skeleton, powerful muscles and particularly keen reflexes make it capable of extraordinary feats. Using its tail as a tightrope walker would use his pole, the cat can regain its balance from the most critical situations. Thus cats have fallen from a height of several storeys without serious injury, when any other land animal would have broken its neck.

and to extend them right out. The strength of its muscles enables it to make giant leaps: indeed, it can reach a height of over 2 metres without taking a run-up. If a tiger could match the domestic cat's performance in proportion, it could jump from the ground to a greater height than the third storey of a building! The cat can achieve such a performance because of very efficient muscles in it hind legs and in its lower back. Its thick, flexible skin which moves freely on its body puts a finishing touch to this miracle of elastic power. The cat's suppleness is useful when recovering from a fall from a great height. The cat's particularly well developed sense of balance, which depends on an extremely flexible tail used for counter-balance, can also enable it to escape unscathed from the most dangerous situations.

Claws and teeth: tools and weapons

Cats walk on their toes and not on the whole sole of their feet. Their powerful claws are retractable – they only extend

when necessary – and cover the toes. Linked to comfortable pads on the bottom of the paws, the claws are used as efficient shock absorbers, so cats can jump from a height without damaging itself. The cat frenetically scratches a tree or a surface in its home to sharpen its claws. They are essential for climbing. Like its teeth, the cat's claws are formidable weapons which enable it to catch and paralyse its prey on the ground. The cat's teeth

Thanks to its powerful claws, the cat can climb trees with great ease.

The cat's fangs are lethal weapons. Its carnivore's dentition enables it to tear meat to pieces once the rasping tongue has finished licking up the blood.

At the sight of a mouse, the cat is capable of transforming itself into a merciless killer, arousing its ferocious instincts.

make it the ultimate predator. A powerful killer, the cat kills in one bite, its carnivore's teeth being designed exclusively for biting and tearing – but not for chewing.

Highly developed senses

Equipped with a highly developed sensory system, the cat is constantly aware of the world around it. The cat's whiskers, which are touch receptors, function like radars. They enable the cat to assess

The domestic cat is as good a hunter as its wild relative.

The cat's sense of hearing is highly developed – more so than its sight or sense of smell. Its hearing enables it to locate its prey or to anticipate danger.

The cat's extensive whiskers are highly receptive sensors.

the height and position of every object and even to detect air movement. Although a cat's sense of smell is hardly used for hunting, it is used to detect the scent of other cats, both male and female. The cat's sense of smell is 30 times more highly developed than that of a human being. As for the ears, these too are very sensitive, and can turn in any direction, making them very useful in detecting both prey and predators.

The adorable face of a kitten masks a future source of terror for birds and mice. At a very early age, the young cat practices its hunting skills on insects.

Despite being exclusively carnivorous, the cat will happily eats grass – it is said to adore barley – with the sole aim of purging itself.

Third eye and sixth sense

Although they cannot see anything in pitch black, cats take advantage of the faintest source of light to pierce the darkness. However, their ability to see in colour is considerably inferior to that of human beings. In any case, efficient night vision is much more important to a nocturnal hunter than the imperfect perception of colours. Cats have the gift of an extra sense which you could call an internal compass that enables them to be sure of finding their

With its pupil at maximum dilation, the cat can perceive the faintest light.

While the lynx's sight is legendary (it can see a waterfowl at 300 metres), the domestic cat, with its pupils of variable geometry can adapt to the intensity of light.

way home. A British cat called Sooty made a 160 kilometre journey from England to Wales to find his ownersí former home – a journey which took six months!

The language of cats

Cats can communicate in a variety of ways. Apart from the voice which can be gentle and purring, or raucous and menacing, the expressions of its features also 'talk'. For example, when the cat shows aggression and

Some cats use their paws to make their demands understood.

The cat expresses anger or fear by flattening its ears back and swishing its tail.

Fur standing on end, arched back, erect tail – everything is ready to impress a potential adversary and make him believe that his opponent is stronger than he actually is.

The cat uses a whole scale of miaows to express itself.

intimidation, its ears flatten backwards, its pupils dilate, its hairs bristle, and its lips draw back to bear its teeth. If the animal is wary, it points its ears forward. To show contentment, the cat will almost close its eyes in an expression of bliss. The whole body also communicates a cat's state of mind: an arched back can be a sign of intimidation, but it can also express the cat's desire to be stroked. A cat that walks at a relaxed pace, with its tail in the air, is self-assured and confident.

Feline territory

The cat attaches great importance to marking its territory, which it does by urinating. It also uses a smelly substance secreted from glands situated on the muzzle, on its temples and under the tail, to stake ownership of an object. It will happily rub against a piece of wood or even a human leg to mark its territory.

The cat's character

Cats have a capacity for mimicry that delights their owners.

It is often said that a domestic cat is independent. Cats are certainly more independent than dogs, but even so, they do seem to enjoy human company. Very playful by nature, the cat belongs to a group of animals which play purely for pleasure. Some scientists regard the cat's play as a repetition of its predatory instincts. This miniature tiger is still undeniably programmed for hunting, and even the best-fed domestic cat feels the need to chase mice, birds, or flies. In an echo of its natural viciousness, the cat 'plays' with its victims and gives the impression of torturing them at its leisure before finally leaving them for dead.

The cat's particularly expressive face has long enthralled humans, who are passionate about this little wildcat around their homes.

Is play a type of hunting, or is hunting a game? Cats are attracted to hiding places such as pipes, tunnels, and dark corners as if wanting to lie in ambush to surprise their prey. Similarly, cats are fascinated by boxes, bags, balls, and pieces of paper. They use these objects as if they were live prey such as mice or birds, subjecting them to the same cruel fate. However, they can suddenly lose interest if something more interesting attracts their attention.

A refined palate

While cats have a reputation for hating water, some won't give a moment's thought to getting wet in order to satisfy their insatiable appetite for fish. They also like mice, birds, and small snakes. A cat can be a very fussy eater if it hasn't had the pleasure of hunting, but it quickly becomes a petty thief, beggar or looter to satisfy its instincts – the cat's meal must be the result of a fight or of effort. Cats only need a small amount of water,

Cats never tire of chasing birds.

Like their big wildcat cousins, cats are mainly active at night. This is not surprising, considering their ability to see in the dark.

A hunter by nature, the cat takes pleasure in breaking the rules – such as stealing food.

most of which is derived from their daily food. With the exception of the Siamese breed, all cats adore cow's milk. However, they have great difficulty in digesting it.

A built-in wash bag

Cleaning is a daily exercise for cats, to which they give considerable attention. Because of its extreme suppleness, the cat can reach all parts of its body. Since its head can turn almost 180 degrees, it can clean its

A mere shadow can spark off the excitement of a game for a cat.

Although cats adore milk, it does not fulfil their dietary needs once they have been weaned.

shoulders with its tongue. It cleans its head with a moistened paw, which it uses like a 'shower mitt'. The tongue is covered in tiny spines which are also used as a comb to untangle the coat and pick up dead hairs on the way.

Cleanliness is essential

The cat is a naturally clean animal, and buries its excrement. Even when living in an apartment, it baulks at using a dirty litter tray.

Cats devote a large proportion of their day to the task of cleaning themselves.

Cats keep themselves in good condition, paying particular attention to their claws, which must always be kept well sharpened.

For the domestic cat, the smallest patch of greenery is a savannah or jungle, where it shows off all of its talents as a miniature wildcat.

This behaviour is rooted in an ancient instinct: wild cats need to take these precautions to remove any trace of their movements, in case of possible enemies. In another context, the mother cat will eat the excrement of her young in order to minimize any risk of parasites in her litter.

Reproduction and the young

While cats' sexual act only lasts a few seconds, the courtship dance which proceeds mating

A mother cat carefully licks its young – even if in fact they're puppies.

Using its tongue, the mother cat cleans her young several times a day, untangling their fur in the process and maintaining their hygiene until they are able to clean themselves.

can last a whole night, accompanied by a great many long raucous, rasping cries which can be heard all around the neighbourhood. A female cat in season is often dramatic, matched by the fighting amongst her suitors. Generally, several competing tom cats surround the receptive female. Bloody battles settle the outcome. During the combat, the female stands to one side, completely preoccupied with cleaning herself. Then, she accepts the advances of the winner

The combat between tom cats is extremely violent.

The female cat indicates that she is in season with her voice, emitting cries and harsh miaows until the males in her entourage respond to her call.

The sexual act between cats is so brief that it can be repeated several times. In every instance, it is the female who decides on the right moment.

The female cat is a very protective mother.

and even two or three competing suitors. Because of her extreme fertility, she can give birth to kittens with different fathers in the same litter.

Maternal love

At birth, the young are both blind and deaf. They remain so for between four and ten days. Usually, there are four kittens to a litter, but there can be as many as a dozen. As with humans, the first milk produced by the mother contains ingredients vital to the kittens' development. The process of weaning the kittens begins after four weeks of a diet consisting exclusively of mother's milk. Weaning is complete at the age of eight weeks. Kittens acquire their mother's antibodies by habitually licking her tongue. During this critical period, the mother may refuse to give milk to one of her offspring, because she has decided that her litter is too large or that one kitten is weaker than the rest. A domestic cat's owners may try to encourage her to continue feeding a kitten, but the mother cat's rejection is unrelenting and merciless. However, a mother cat's capacity for love can be immense, to the extent that they have been known to raise orphan kittens or even to bring up the young of another species such as dogs or rats. At the age of ten weeks, the young kitten is capable of cleaning itself. Previously, of course, it was the mother who was responsible for cleaning her young. It is now time to play, and the kittens will venture further and further away from the safety of their basket in order to discover and explore the outside world.

All kittens have blue eyes at first, and are blind at birth.

From the age of three months, mischievous kittens give their mother a great deal of work, she can no longer keep them in their nest except when it is time for a nap or for feeding.

▼ Play for kittens is a real school for life. They use play to practise hunting, making a ball roll with their paw which they pursue carefully and then 'kill' viciously. Through play, the mischievous kitten will incidentally pick up certain skills such as opening a cupboard door. During the course of play, young cats also start to appreciate that they must be wary when faced with danger. They must also learn to use their teeth and claws as weapons.

With their refined elegance, the Angoras have exquisitely soft fur. They are descended from a very old Turkish breed.

Persian and other long-haired cats

The family of long-haired cats owes its worldwide success to the Persian, the unrivalled star of high society drawing rooms for centuries. Less well known are the Angoras and the Birman – yet they have their own unique charm and can challenge the Persian in the seduction stakes.

The Persian was introduced into Europe at the beginning of the 18th century. Since then, its success with its admirers has not waned.

In the category of long-haired cats, the best known are the so-called 'Persians'. In Britain, the Persian is usually called the Longhair, the name 'Persian' only being given to 'Self' cats (those with a coat of one colour). Many cat lovers consider them to be the most beautiful specimens of the feline race. However, the Turkish Angoras, the Birman, the Himalayans and the Chinchillas, all possess potent powers of seduction. According to the whims of fashion, one

The Persian's tortoiseshell coat is no obstacle to entering competitions.

Advances in the field of genetics have enabled humans to develop new breeds of Persian cats. Whatever the colour of the coat, it is always the type which counts in competitions.

Although the Persian is often confined to the living room, like any other cat, it enjoys frolicking in the garden, concentrating its energies on hunting mice and birds.

or other of the breeds takes the limelight in cat shows. Their silky coat is their trump card.

Persians and Chinchillas

The Persian is traditionally the aristocrat amongst pedigree cats. Its massive, round head and prominent forehead crowned with hair, make it look like an imitation lion. Its short, wide, flattened nose is the distinguishing sign of its Persian lineage. A thick neck, small ears surrounded by a thick tuft of fur

Large, round, almost orange eyes are a typical Persian trait.

The Chinchilla is a superstar. With its green eyes, it combines the physical characteristics of the Persian with the misty softness of the Angora's fur.

Some people believe that the Persian has Slavic origins, although they agree that its first recorded appearance was in Asia Minor. Introduced into Europe in the 18th century by travellers trading with the Orient, the Persian has since conquered the entire planet. Queen Victoria made the Blue Persian fashionable by owning two. The variety of Pekinese Persians look like the dogs of the same name. Incidentally, the Persian cat can be deaf at birth, like certain types of Angora.

The masterful Persian's thick fur is astonishing.

and large, round eyes add to its elegant appearance. The body is stocky, covered in thick fur which lengthens into a mane up to the chest. The Persian, which has a reputation as a placid cat, demands a great deal of care and affection from its owners. The Chinchilla is similar to the Persian. With a more delicate appearance, it sports a magnificent silvery white coat and big emerald green eyes, which contribute to its popularity with cat lovers.

The Turkish Angora

Neglected, yet representing one of the oldest breeds of long-haired domestic cats, the Angora enjoyed a revival in the 1970s when American breeders took an interest in it. This elegant feline, which originated around Lake Van in Turkey, had nearly disappeared, replaced in cat lovers' affections by the Persian. An agile cat with long, slim limbs, it has soft, thick fur, an angular head, large ears and almond-shaped eyes. The Angora is an intelligent cat which can be trained to perform tricks. Unusually for a cat, it loves bathing.

The Birman

A variant of the Angora, the Turkish van is a cat which can tolerate water!

This fashionable cat was kept in the temples of Burma – hence its alternative name, the Sacred Cat of Burma. Specialists believe it guarded the entrances to holy places and was an object of worship. It nearly disappeared during World War II when its meat was valued by people suffering from starvation. The intense blue of its large eyes give it a bewitching gaze. Its short legs end in white gauntlets and its luxuriant fur is

The Birman is a majestic cat whose silky fur is the equal of other long- or semi-longhaired cats.

The Himalayan, halfway between the Persian and the Birman, is a splendid cat whose type was officially accepted in the USA at the end of the 1930s.

coloured around the ears and the tail. An extrovert cat, its sexual temperament seems highly developed

The Himalayan

The Himalayan's long hair make it appear adapted for endless snow. The reason for its appearance is more prosaic: this cat was created by crossing Persians and Siamese – a genetic invention created entirely by humans. It is a cat renowned for docility.

The Birman's blue eyes could be those of the goddess Tsun-Kyan-Kse ...

Extremely extrovert – its detractors even say it is emotionally disturbed – the Siamese is an extraordinary lively cat which fears nothing.

Oriental cats and Siamese

Oriental cats are characterized by their slim, narrow figure. With high limbs and a short coat, they carry a triangular head perched on a long neck with great nobility. Among the breeds of cat that are gifted acrobats and very talkative, the Siamese is without doubt one of the world's favourite cats.

Siamese cats often establish a special relationship with their owners to the point of exclusivity, leaving little room for those who might disturb this harmony.

With a reputation for intelligence, faithfulness and exclusivity, the cat of Oriental origin is the most sought after of the so-called short-haired cats. Very active and excessively voluble, it takes over the whole house and its inhabitants.

The Siamese

Like a ballet dancer perched on long legs, walking as though on tiptoe, the Siamese is one of the most refined

The comfort-loving Siamese likes cosy places.

The variants of coat colour in Siamese do not affect their general appearance, which must be slim and energetic.

Curious about every thing and attentive to the territory which they have chosen to share with humans, Siamese cats react to the slightest unusual sound.

The Siamese has blue, almond-shaped eyes.

breeds of cat. Its head is topped by large ears which widen at the base. The size, shape and position of its eyes match its 'Oriental' looks. Its blue eyes and beige coat, set off by a dark mask give it a certain style, especially as the ends of its feet, ears and tail match this darker colouring. Its hair is so short and fine that its musculature is revealed with each of its movements. The Siamese has a reputation for jealousy and is renowned for its legendary dexterity.

Several varieties of Siamese

There are several breeds of cat that are comparable in every way to the Siamese, except for their coat. Thus the Balinese and its variant, the Javanese, are the result of expert crossings between several Siamese which eventually have created a 'long hair' gene. In reality, these cats have a thicker coat than the Siamese but it is nothing like the coat of their Burmese cousins. The short-haired Oriental is a 'Self' (single-colour) version of the Siamese.

The Havana Brown is distinguished by its large ears and chocolate colouring.

Like the Siamese, the short-haired Oriental, although blessed with an easy-going character, demands a lot of attention from its owners. All the so-called 'Oriental' cats have a reputation for being noisy – especially the female, who, when in season, cries to her suitors for hours in an extremely shrill voice that many human beings find unbearable.

The Burmese

A purely American product, the Burmese is Burmese only in name. Stockier than the Siamese, it is also more

Enjoying direct contact with their peers, Siamese cats are very playful by nature, which is expressed by play fights and endless races.

▼ All Burmese of the world are proud descendants of Wong Mau, a cat brought from the former French province of Tonkin to the USA by a Dr Thompson in the 1930's. Crossbred with a Siamese, Wong Mau gave birth to a sepia-coloured kitten. Burmese were at first refused by feline clubs before they were finally allowed to enter competition in 1953. Since then they have been showing together with other cats whose fur is of a sable, sepia-blue, chocolate or lilac colour.

The Bombay is descended from a Burmese crossed with an American black cat.

powerfully built. With this cat, everything seems round: the head, the forehead and the muzzle, which is astonishingly short for a cat of Oriental origin. Its eyes arc golden in colour and its fur is thick and shiny, caught between shades of sepia and mahogany. More 'civilized' than the Siamese, the Burmese is renowned for having a sense of humour.

The Bombay

The Bombay gets its name

The Red Siamese appeared in breeding during the 1960s, a time when the phenomenal Siamese craze reached its height.

Far from the concerns of the beauty contests organized by humans, the Siamese cat takes natural advantage of its elegance.

from its resemblance to the black panther of India. Its shiny ebony coat has an unusual appearance like that of polished leather. This solid cat has a highly developed musculature and is surprisingly heavy considering its size. Even-tempered and affectionate, the Bombay is a trouble-free cat.

The Abyssinian, the Oriental from Africa

With its finely marked coat, the Abyssinian resembles a large

The Abyssinian cat, with its fawn coat, looks like a small puma.

Sure of its balance, the Somalian is an expert climber. Inquisitive yet at the same time cautious, the Somalian takes care to move without disturbing anything in its path.

The origins of the Abyssinian are unknown. The only certainty is that the lineage of this majestic cat is very old.

The Somalian, with its thick fur, can tolerate extreme cold.

wildcat – in miniature form. Many specialists consider the Abyssinian to be a direct descendant of the Ancient Egyptian pharoahs' sacred cat. However, there is no proof of this royal lineage and the Abyssinian simply seems to be the wildest of the domestic cats. Its large, almond-shaped eyes, and natural elegance encourage comparisons with the Orientals. The Abyssinian is adventurous and is not particularly scared of dogs. Somalians are long-haired Abyssinians. Their athleticism makes them seem like small wildcats.

If the dog is considered to be man's best friend, man is unquestionably the cat's best friend, chosen by the cat according to its own criteria!

European and other cats of the world

Whether wild or domesticated, the vast majority of moggies around the world are mongrel cats. The definition 'European cat' has given humans the freedom to develop very 'naturalistic' cats. Consequently, some very strange breeds have been created.

Capable of independence regardless of any obstacles in its ways, the domestic cat takes advantage of what seem to be resources left at his disposal by humans.

The feline world would be a sad place without its most promiscuous citizen, the common cat, otherwise known as the alley cat. The so-called 'European' cats, which ultimately are close relations of the moggie, have further diversified the huge spectrum of pedigree cats. Thanks to cross-breeding and the mysterious workings of genetics, some incredible strains of cat have come into existence – sometimes very remote from the archetypal Egyptian Mau,

It takes very little to bring out the highly playful nature in kittens.

Whatever its shape or colour, the common cat can easily be compared in terms of elegance with its so-called pedigree cousins.

A fighter and a rebel, only needing humans when it wants a good, long stroke, the alley cat is certainly the only animal to have domesticated its owner.

which is thought to be the direct descendant of the African Wildcat, *Felis sylvestris libyca.*

The Egyptian Mau

Although it could be mistaken for the cats depicted in the rich iconography of the pyramids, the Mau, which is found nowadays mainly in Europe and the United States, is the result of different cross-breeding during the 20th century. This unusual breed has a brown coat, and whether the coat has silvering or a dark smoke, it is always

The Egyptian Mau is one of the most refined breeds in the world.

The present-day Egyptian Mau is a descendant of Baba, a female cat given by the Egyptian ambassador to Italy to Princess Troubetskoy, who lived in Rome at the start of the 1950s.

The ultimate example of a cat without controlled breeding, the European domestic cat, commonly known as the alley cat, represents the majority of the world's cats. Even when it has not found a home to its liking, it lives freely amongst human beings, and reproduces very easily through random encounters. Mixtures and hybrids of all types give it an unrivalled genetic richness. The variety of sizes, colours, builds, and coats seen in these cats is endless, and the enclosed world of cat competitions has at last opened its doors to them.

The Chartreux is a big blue-grey cat with golden eyes.

spotted. Its wide, round eyes are a magnificent gooseberry shade of green. They intensify the Mau's expression of perpetual surprise. The Mau walks like a panther, with its slender, athletic body. Indeed, with features such as its surprisingly long hind legs, the Mau's talents as a sprinter are beyond dispute. The Mau is reserved in temperament, only expressing happiness to its owner. It does so like a dog, by wagging its tail.

The Chartreux

Of French origin, this blue cat was created in the tranquillity of the abbeys of Carthusian monks. Heavily built, its stocky body and robust chest contrast with short, relatively slender legs. The mocking expression of the Chartreux soon gave rise to the nickname 'smiling cat'. Its thick fur, extremely soft to touch, is of one colour, and sometimes has a silvery sheen. Although gentle by nature, this cat is a formidable hunter of rodents, and has often been kept as a rat catcher.

The Russian Blue

This cat, another blue, probably originated in Russia. Legend

has it that it was brought to western Europe by Russian sailors during the middle of the 19th century. Its short, thick, silky fur can be likened to a beaver's coat. Its hairs are silver-tipped, which gives its coat a magnificent sheen, complemented with green eyes. The Russian Blue is also distinguishable from other blue cats by its incredibly soft, almost inaudible voice. A cat with a rather timid disposition, it will only be expressive with its owner.

The Russian Blue is a reclusive, loyal companion.

The short-haired cat (English or American) is an engaging animal which does not miaow much but purrs frequently, as it is extremely affectionate.

The non-pedigree European cat shows disdain for the standards which bring happiness to cat lovers. It gets on with its life, competitions or no competitions.

The Maine Coon

Of unknown origin, this giant American cat is said to be a cross between a wildcat and a racoon – despite all evidence to the contrary. Apart from this amusing legend, the Maine Coon is one of the largest domestic cats in the world. Usually tabby, its fur is quite thick, which puts it in the category of medium long-haired cats. A mixture of elegance and toughness, this animal is very friendly and can thrive in harsh climates.

The Maine Coon could be described as a fake lynx. It can weigh up to 10 kilograms.

The Norwegian Forest Cat

This close relative of the Maine Coon has very hot fur, as well as a robust build and long hind legs which enable it to jump very high, climb trees without difficulty, and move with ease through snow. The Norwegian is a rural cat which loves open spaces, and is not afraid of water. Reputed to have a high IQ, it is not any the less faithful for being bright, and sometimes it can be extremely attached to its owner.

The sturdy Norwegian Forest Cat or Skogkatt has water-repellent fur.

The Manx

Originating on the Isle of Man, the Manx is tailless. In this respect, it is similar to the Japanese Bobtail, which only has a short pom-pom for a tail. Like all cats living in cold, difficult climatic conditions, the Manx has a very thick double coat. Apart from the strange absence of a tail, the Manx is notable for ears, which are angled outwards.

The Rex

There are two types of Rex: the Cornish Rex with its curly coat, and the Devon Rex, which could be mistaken for a bat

During the 1000 years that it has existed in Japan, the Bobtail, with its short tail rolled up into a little pom-pom, is associated with omens of good fortune and happiness.

▼ The Scottish Fold has its origins in a spontaneous mutation which occurred in Scotland. It is the only cat in the world which possesses folded ears, resembling small hoods. Its round silhouette makes it look slightly fat. It has big and round eyes and a short and thick fur which may take a variety of colours: brown, blue or white; and self-coloured, striped or shadowed. There is also a long-haired Scottish Fold with the same characteristics.

The origins of the Manx have long captured people's imaginations. It is said that it swam ashore to the Isle of Man during the 16th century, surviving the shipwreck of a ship belonging to the invincible Armada.

because of its enormous ears. It is said that these two bizarre breeds of cat, with their very short, fine hair, suit cat lovers who suffer the misfortune of being allergic to cats.

The Sphinx

A completely bald, wrinkled cat, nicknamed 'the E.T. of felines', the Sphinx is definitely the strangest breed of cats. Love it or loathe it, no-one can be indifferent to it.

It is said at competitions that the Sphinx has the traits of a monkey, a dog, and a cat.

The Devon Rex is an incredible cat whose short, almost curly coat can have the texture of the finest velvet.

Part two

Cats in Our World

27820

Entering long ago into the pantheon of ancient Egypt, the cat took pride of place on the funeral steles of the Middle Empire, about 2000 BC.

The cat's divine attributes

Whether depicted as a mysterious guardian at the gates of night, or believed to be a representation of Bastet, the goddess of fertility, the cat was regarded as a sacred animal by the Ancient Egyptians. It was also considered to be a good spirit, both in the Roman Empire and in the Gallo-Roman civilization.

The cat's timeless profile always suggests its divine nature even if it has deserted the gentle twilight of the banks of the Nile.

The subject of worship since its domestication by humans, the cat has in turn been associated with the creation myths, with guardian angels, then with moon or sun goddesses. Following the cat's gradual integration into the everyday life of ancient peoples because of its natural talents as a mouser, all kinds of powers were soon attributed to it, including the ability to influence destiny. The unfathomable mystery of the cat's gaze, the beauty of its eyes glinting in the dark, its independence and

The Egyptian Mau is the closest descendent of the pharaohs' cats.

It takes more than silk cushions and gilt to impress the Egyptian cat, which has been used to the luxury reserved for gods since the earliest Antiquity.

In ancient Egypt, the female cat was almost raised to the rank of weaning mother, protecting the new-born, artists, and doctors.

habitual nocturnal expeditions have made the cat worthy of human admiration. The calming effect and sense of well-being that a cat brings to a house have given rise to beliefs in its supernatural ancestry.

The relationship between humans and felines has a long history

The oldest remains of domestic cats were discovered at the site of Jericho, in Palestine, and date back to 6700 BC. Later, the first representations of the cat were

Bastet is a vengeful lioness who became a feline protector.

conceived as wall paintings, statuettes, and the mummies of ancient Egypt. About four or five thousand years ago, wild cats from the desert appeared in the Nile valley, probably attracted by the rodents that devoured human grain stores. We can assume that farmers of the era tamed this predator for the great talents it exhibited in defending their precious crops. Cats soon did well out of the situation, particularly as they quickly became the objects of devout worship. Who knows who adopted whom, the cat or the human?

The entrance to the Cat Museum at Basel (Switzerland) evokes the Egyptian Bastet.

The cat of antiquity

Dating from 2000 BC, the first paintings of cats bear witness to their importance in the everyday life of every Egyptian citizen. They have been found in the pharoahs' tombs and in those of important figures in society. It was during this era that the cat became associated with the goddess Hathor. According to legend, Queen Tiy, wife of Amenhotep III (1408–1372 BC) showed unequalled adoration of her cat, at a time when some Egyptian high dignitaries went as far as keeping sarcophaguses for their favourite animals.

The high dignitaries of ancient Egypt thought nothing of mummifying their favourite cats, giving them funerals worthy of their rank in society.

During the New Empire (around 1000 BC), Egyptian noblemen in the Thebes region enjoyed bird hunting as a favourite pastime. During the tracking of birds in the high grass lining the Nile marshes, cats were a most helpful ally for retrieving game. The faithful companion followed its master even in death. The walls of a number of tombs depict scenes of bird hunting showing cats and their masters in the pursuit of their common passion.

The feline incarnation of the goddess Bastet

With the advent of the cat-goddess Bastet, the cat acquired its definitive status as a sacred animal in Egypt. This deity, with a woman's body and a cat's head, was the guardian of the royal children. Subsequently, her blessing was extended to all new-born babies. Bastet's twin sister Sekhmet was the goddess of war and destruction. Bastet also symbolised fertility; promoted to the rank of mother-goddess, she

In Egypt the cat naturally found its place in the courts of the most powerful.

Sacred in status, the Egyptian female cat is synonymous with life, and its legendary fertility raised it to the rank of mother goddess.

The worship devoted to Bastet, practised principally in Bubastis during the New Empire (around 1000 BC), has bequeathed a rich statuary of Egyptian cats.

Whether living or commemorated as a statue, cats were venerated all over Egypt.

eventually became the guardian of music, dance, and medicine.

The cat: victim of its own success

By the time the city of Bubastis became the Egyptian capital around 950 BC Bastet was the most important deity in Egypt, attracting hundreds of thousands of pilgrims every spring. In the most secluded recesses of the temple built in honour of the goddess, priests tended sacred cats, which were

Perfectly integrated into the daily existence of Egyptians, cats were protected, and to attempt to kill them was regarded as one of the most heinous of crimes.

placed in sarcophaguses after their deaths – like kings. One less savoury aspect of the cult of Bastet was that kittens were strangled and embalmed wholesale. They were then sold at the temple entrance by pedlars to pilgrims who wanted the blessings of the goddess to be bestowed on them, but lacked offerings.

The Cat of Light

The Egyptians also worshipped the Great Cat or Cat of Light.

The unfathomable expression of a cat's eyes adds to its mystery.

With its noble and occasionally haughty expression, the cat enjoys domestic comfort and soon shows who is the master, even god, of the house.

In the bestiary of Egyptian gods, the sphinx, with a man's head and feline body, has an undeniable relationship to Bastet, the cat-goddess.

According to the *Book of the Dead*, this animal lived with the sun god Ra, Bastet's father. Every night, the cat fought with Apep, the evil snake of the darkness. Having won the fight, the Cat of Light cut off the snake of darkness's head. Consequently the sun, symbolized by a boat, could continue on its course and day could break at last. Considering it's key role in this legend, it is understandable why the cat enjoyed the status of a protected animal. Killing a cat was

Urns and sarcophaguses illustrated with cats were part of funeral rites.

Apart from its mystical aspect, the Egyptian cat also inspired fables in which its talents as a guardian and hunter were celebrated.

In Peru, representations of deified cats have been found, which proved their importance from about 600 BC onwards.

In many civilizations, the cat is held to be a friend of the gods. Thus, in the Roman empire the animal was a symbol of fertility andaccompanied children to the afterlife. In Arabia, the prophet Mohammed once cut off a part of his coat rather than disturb his cat dozing on it. In India, China and Japan, cats have always been mythical animals. They are tokens of prosperity and keep bad spirits at bay.

The Chinese ideogram signifying cat does not lack movement nor a sense of speed.

punishable by the death penalty, and according to the Greek author Diodorus, a passing Roman was hung because he was responsible for the accidental death of a cat. The historian Herodotus reports that during a fire, it was more important to save cats than to put out the fire! If someone suffered the misfortune of a cat dying in their home, its owners shaved off their eyebrows as a mark of mourning.

The valiant cat

Such overwhelming love for the cat led to the downfall of ancient Egypt. Cambysces II, the king of Persia in 525 BC had a keen insight into this phenomenon. His soldiers bound cats to their shields, so the Egyptians surrendered without a fight, immobilized by the sight of such sacrilege. More recently, cats continued to take part in wars. During World War II, a cat on board a British boat ignored its wounds and continued catching rats on the vessel, thus saving the crew's food supplies. He was awarded the Dikin Medal for this noble deed, a medal reserved for the bravest of the brave!

The black cat was annihilated because it was suspected of being in league with the devil.
It made a successful comeback at the beginning of the 20th century.

Feline devilry

During the Middle Ages, cats, especially black cats, acquired a reputation tainted with a whiff of brimstone. With their nocturnal habits, it was not long before these independent creatures epitomized all kinds of irrational fears. Their association with witches led to their demise, burned at the stake as victims of human prejudice.

The occasionally worried expression on a cat's face, its searching look, and above all the lack of understanding by humans gave rise to the cat's persecution over a long period.

Through no fault of its own, a number of supernatural, even evil powers were attributed to the cat. These beliefs are reflected in the multitude of proverbs in which the cat plays a malevolent role. In its tortuous relationship with the human race, the cat gradually lost all of the advantages that it had gained in Antiquity. A scapegoat for every human misfortune, the little feline, which thrived in the countryside as well as in towns, would soon find it almost impossible to

A lover of heat, the cat got so close to the human hearth that it got burnt.

With its eyes full of mystery and its bewitching look, as if detached from the world which surrounds it, the cat was an ideal vector to embody the devil.

In the imagination and the tradition of folk tales and legends, the cat, which can see at night, and is not afraid of dark forests, awakens all the fears of childhood.

shake off its association with the occult. Although as a rat catcher the cat was the first credible line of defence against the great plagues that afflicted the world during the Middle Ages, it was suspected of making the most atrocious pacts imaginable with the devil.

Sayings and superstitions

From then on, the cat and the strange powers bestowed on it were embroiled with a large number of superstitions, some of which survive today. When a cat

Could the black coat of an adorable kitten be the garment of Satan!

A cat deserting the house of a sick person was interpreted as the omen of an imminent death.

puts its paw behind its ear or when it sneezes, some people still believe that this is a portent of rain. In another context, anyone whose path is crossed by a black cat coming from the left can expect terrible misfortune, and if the unfortunate encounter takes place at the crossroads of four forest paths around midnight, the calamity will be even worse. Young women who accidentally tread on a cat's tail – whatever the cat's colour – will be condemned to spinsterhood for a number of years corresponding

Giving the frog a run for its money when it comes to weather forecasting, the cat announces the arrival of a storm by touching its ear with its paw.

Frequenting human cemeteries, the cat knows better than anyone how to enjoy the calm and serenity of places where its nap is unlikely to be disturbed.

to the number of times that the animal howls. In a more tragic role, the cat can also be associated with death. For example in Tuscany, when a mortal curse is put on someone, Death appears to the victim in the form of a cat.

The sworn enemy of the church

The first signs of mistrust towards the cat appeared in the seventh century AD. From this time onwards, the papacy threw scorn on the cat, accusing it of

Accused of devilry, the cat has often been banished from human society.

being Satan's henchman. It was also associated with women's fertility and, by extension with the moon. The church looked unfavourably on the remnants of a pagan world, and its main aim was to stamp them out to assert its power. From the 13th century onwards, the poor mouse-catcher was itself hunted down – by humans.

The feline heretic

Serious allegations that the cat was in league with the devil were made in connection with the papal prosecution of heretics. Pope Gregory IX, who has the dubious distinction of organizing the Inquisition, gave an account of gruesome witches' sabbaths in a papal bull. He said that Lucifer appeared to Christian sects considered by the papacy to be heretical, such as the Cathars or Waldensians. They were accused of worshipping the devil in the form of a black cat, a symbol of lewdness, of temptations of the flesh and of ungodly worship. The cat became the focus of the most sacrilegious rituals imaginable. Often described or depicted in poses suggesting lust – for example with the tail erect, showing its genitals – the cat

Courageous cats don't even fear fire!

The most evil of all, the black cat is the indispensable complement to old spell books and flying brooms for anyone trying the charms of witchcraft.

With the exception of England where they are supposed to bring luck, black cats had — and still have — a diabolical reputation which once led to their relentless persecution and almost to their extinction. The victim of these widespread superstitions sometimes only survived owing to particular marks, like a tuft of white hair at its neck, the so-called 'angel's mark', whereas its more unfortunate mates did not escape death.

No true witch would be complete without a cat, broom, owl, and bat.

represented femininity, a quality judged to be impure and immodest at the time.

Sacrifices and barbarity

Campaigns were orchestrated against the cat to exorcise the evil which it embodied. It was a time of sacrifices and stakes which lasted for centuries. These dubious practices were linked to the agrarian rites which marked the rhythm of the year, and the massacre of cats took place on set dates, on religious feast days. For

A silent witness to the demonic activities of its mistress, the cat, and its natural secrecy, is the ideal companion for any self-respecting sorceress.

To get to the Sabbath rites, one of the best means of transport used in the community of devil worshippers is the cat: rapid, quiet, and comfortable.

example on St John's Day, corresponding with the summer solstice, a stake lit by the King of France himself was erected at the Place de Grève, the main square of Paris. Dozens of live cats trapped in sacks were consigned to the flames. At Ypres, in Belgium, cats were thrown from the top of the town's belfry during the second week of Lent. A stop was put to these strange feline flying lessons as late as 1817, and fortunately the custom has now been replaced by symbolically throwing stuffed toy cats from

Before the Sabbath, witches smear themselves with ointments made from feline fat.

Ferocious and pitiless at times like these, the cat, which can also retract its claws and charm people by purring, exhibits a disturbing split personality.

the belfry. In other countries such as Germany or England, where water was the preferred means of execution rather than air or fire, cats were put to death by drowning.

A good or evil spirit?

It was quite common practice to brick up a cat in the foundations of a house. The custom derived from a piece of folk wisdom that held that a cat embodied a good spirit. In France, Belgium, and England, the remains of cats

Darkness is not essential to see the cat's diabolical smile.

were discovered in the foundations of many old buildings. The purpose behind this custom was to ensure the long life and prosperity of the inhabitants of the building in which the sacrifice had taken place.

The cat and the witch

The diabolical image of the cat during the Middle Ages was associated with witches from the 15th century onwards. These women, who were the most frequent practitioners of traditional

The cat accompanies the witch wherever she goes.

A black cat playing in a garden, a reminder of the presence of evil to damned souls, condemned never to know respite.

rural medicine, were singled out by academics and the clergy. Interrogated under torture, these women confessed to being able to turn themselves into cats with ease in order to devote themselves more effectively to their rites. Indeed, like cats, witches display most of their talents by night. Like the cat, the witch is independent, rebellious, and has often been accused of exhibiting excessive eroticism. The link with the cat was therefore obvious, and a great number of these women's lives ended at the stake for the sole crime of keeping a cat.

The proximity of a Chartreux and a broom could be a sign of the presence of evil.

Cats, born actors and expiatory victims of witchcraft were associated with the most evil bacchanalian rites observed in honour of the devil.

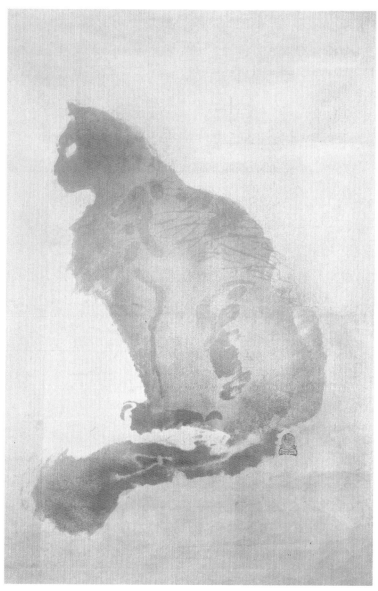

Harmless little devil or true demon? The cat, with its eyes like burning coals, its pointed ears and paws equipped with claws, is a bit of both. It depends how you look at it.

During the art deco period at the beginning of the 20th century, many artists became passionate about the cat, which was an endless source of inspiration.

The cat in art and literature

During the 17th century, the aristocracy and in turn the middle classes rediscovered the cat and made it fashionable. Indeed, the graceful feline became the darling of literary salon. In the 19th and 20th centuries, poets, and writers felt so passionately about cats that they featured them in their work.

The Renaissance marked the beginning of the cat's return to favour in the West. Having been persecuted during the Middle Ages, it regained its status of family pet through art.

From the end of the Renaissance, then during the 16th and 17th centuries, the cat gradually regained its status as a domestic animal. The great epidemics of Black Death (bubonic plague) which devastated Europe played no small part in this turnaround in its fortune. The cat regained its importance because it was the only known enemy of rats, the principal means by which the plague was spread. The cat's rehabilitation was also due to the sudden passion devoted to it.

The artist seized upon the idea of the symbolic man-cat with enthusiasm.

Paintings of everyday life in the 18th century gave a favourable role to the cat, an impenitent hunter of mice, in the existence of humans.

During the 15th century, the cat began to regain its place beside the dog in the domestic environment of humans.

The cat's come-back

Famous men enjoyed feline company, such as Cardinal Richelieu, Louis XIII's chief minister, who adored tiny kittens and he left a tidy sum to his cats in his will, so that they could be cared for after his death. The cat took advantage of the new feline fad to reclaim its place in even the most modest of homes, particularly in England. The aristocracy continued to confer the rank of nobility on the cat. For example, Madame de La

Some cats even inherited their owners fortunes during the 17th century.

The painters of the 19th century managed to capture perfectly the moments of intimacy shared by cats and humans.

Sablière, patroness of the poet Jean de La Fontaine, having withdrawn into a convent, only kept her favourite tomcat by her side for company. During the following century, cats were the focus of every form of human fascination, especially intellectual enquiry, in literary salons. Many society women gathered men of letters, men of science, and aristocrats around them, imposing their little companion on their guests, who was now raised to regal rank on the divan. They would

For Jean de La Fontaine's mice distrust is the mother of safety.

willingly leave their fortunes, servants, and houses to their cats, to the great displeasure of the legitimate heirs.

Cats in literature

The cat's haughty temperament, its distant, even enigmatic manner, its indomitable spirit evoking fantasies of freedom, inspired and charmed generations of writers of the era. The commonplace association of the cat with the solitary person dipping the quill or pounding away at the

Children consider the cat as a confidant who will not betray their secrets.

The author Colette, who shared her life and work with her cats, was happy to appear on the stage at the BaTaClan to play the part of a cat herself. The cat in love.

Pussy cat, Pussy cat, where have you been? The folk tales illustrated by Kate Greenway enjoyed great success in London at the beginning of the 20th century.

In painting, the cat's suppleness, its lithe body, and the aesthetic of its movements have often inspired the great master painters. Leonardo de Vinci included a cat and her kittens in his sketches for the Madonna and Child. The cat also fascinated artists such as Dürer, and later Watteau, Chardin, or Manet. In the latter's work, the cat has obviously erotic connotations. Other artists such as Cocteau were interested in cats, as well as Leonor Fini, for whom the cat took on a symbolic aspect.

Charles Perrault's *Puss in Boots* has captured children's imagination.

keyboard was created by poets and writers themselves, as the cat is the hero of countless literary works. In literature, the little feline is endowed with angelic traits or depicted as deceitful or cruel. Such variety in its portrayal bears witness to the important position which the cat holds in the company of men of letters, being his equal, or at least his friend.

Fables and Tales

Popular literature abounds with stories about cats, with the classic *Puss in Boots* being the most notable example. Originally an Italian folk tale, *Puss in Boots* was rewritten by Charles Perrault in 1697. The story gave the cat a new dimension, portraying it as a brilliant ambassador to the good and the great. For Jean de La Fontaine, the Attila of rats' is primarily a cunning hunter who only follows his stomach's counsel. The writer most renowned for taking the cat to Olympian heights in his literature is without any doubt François-Augustin Paradis de Montcrif with his work *The Cats*, which was given a mauling by the critics. Their derision was

The cat did not escape the talented attention of the impressionist painters.

matched by Voltaire, who called him a historiogriffe, a pun on the words historiographer' and griffe', the French word for claw.

The cat, the romantics, and the 20th century

The romantic era is a rich store of references to the cat. Now the cat was admired for the very mysterious, morbid qualities which had caused it to be hated and burned centuries before. *The Black Cat* by Edgar Allan Poe is the

Modern painting has celebrated the cat in all of its movements. Even asleep, it can become the main theme in a master's canvas.

Gustav Klimt (1862–1918), a painter who was one of the main exponents of the Secessionist movement in Vienna, poses with his cat in front of his workshop in 1912.

best example of this admiration. Charles Baudelaire expressed fascination for cats, and Honoré de Balzac used the animal in *The Heartbreak of an English Cat* as a pretext for a satirical story. More recently, other writers have given excellent descriptions of the cat, such as Patricia Highsmith, the American queen of crime, not forgetting the eccentricities of Lewis Carrol.

The cat in music

It is said that the cat's

Henri Rousseau conveyed the affection that author Pierre Loti felt for Pat, his cat.

Paint and cats suit each other's company. When they are not dipping their paws into paint to sign their favourite work, cats can suddenly become artists' models.

Cats have an ear for music, according to musicians. That may be the case, but the concert given by a female cat in season can be intolerable.

In the *The Aristocats* cartoon, the Disney studios created a musician cat.

sense of hearing is very finely tuned. Furthermore, the scale of sounds which it uses in its singing exercises consists of 60 miaowing tones. With its unquestionable sensitivity to music, the cat has charmed a great many musicians, who have associated it with their works. Prominent examples include Chopin's Cat Waltz, Satie's Cat's Song, Ravel's famous feline duet *The Child and its Spells*, inspired by a short story by Colette, or even Rossini in a bravura passage for soprano entitled *The Cats' Duet*.

Whether promoting milk, tobacco or cars, the cat became a symbol of advertising as long ago as the first advertisements, and is still used to suggest home comforts.

The cat, a star among humans

Today's cat has found its niche in society. A peaceful pasha ruling thousands of homes, it is pampered by humans anxious to satisfy its slightest whims. The hero of comic strips and cartoons, the cat has also become a star of the silver screen.

A superhero, *Felix the Cat* has delighted generations of humans in comic strips and cartoons.

All around the world, the cat reigns as absolute master of the house. This is particularly true in western homes. For cat lovers, it is no longer a question of considering the cat as an insignificant domestic animal: no expense is spared when it comes to keeping it happy, and no-one takes stock of the amount of attention lavished on it either.

As the centre of attention in the home, the four-legged hero cannot fail to charm.

In *The Spy With Velvet Paws*, the real star is a Siamese cat.

Cats have conquered Hollywood, which pays homage to them with the School for Cats, the only one of its kind in the world, which was founded in the sprawling city of Los Angeles.

Catwoman, alias Michel Pfeiffer in the film *Batman*, represents the ultimate seductress whom no-one can resist.

Some Cat Statistics

It is impossible to quantify the world's cat population. How-ever, we can try to put forward some figures, especially when it comes to cat ownership in the industrialized countries. The number of cats living in French homes, for instance, exceeds 8 million – a statistic backed up by some very respectable cat fanciers' associations. Cat ownership in France has been on a constant increase since the beginning of the 1990s – even the dog population has been

For James Bond, diamonds are forever for Persian cats.

In periods of abundance, the cat reveals a very discerning palate.

outnumbered. It is also known that 25.5 percent of French households has a cat, and the proportion of the family budget allocated to it is by no means insignificant 2.2 percent of the household income !

A refined gourmet

Consequently, the feline market has proved to be very buoyant, and the pet food industry has not missed out on the trend, stepping up advertising campaigns aimed at cat owners. As the feline palate is particularly

Cats will never exchange their legendary independence for the guarantee of a meal. Even when well fed, they find it hard to resist the appeal of dustbins.

A lover of gardens and flower-strewn steps, where it can practise its hunter's instincts on a careless butterfly, the cat also enjoys long naps in the sun.

refined, special laboratories have been established to conduct rigorous behavioural studies with taster cats'. All of their taste perceptions are given in-depth analysis in order to perfect recipes designed to please the greatest number of cats possible. This seems to satisfy its customers, as 90 percent of owners in first world countries regularly use ready-made cat food.

The cat as supermodel

The cat is also the focus of attention in exhibitions with an

Despite its robust constitution, the cat sometimes needs to visit the vet.

exclusively feline theme. The first cat competition was organized in London in 1871, by a cat lover by the name of Harrison Weir. He was the first person to devise standards for breeds shown in competitions, based on precise criteria. Whereas at that time the colour and the pattern of the fur were sufficient to define a breed of cat, these days the characteristics that merit the label pedigree have become much more complicated. Nowadays, rearing and cross-breeding take into account all of the progress made by geneticists, and breeders can invent new types of cat by selecting the physiological features that interest them.

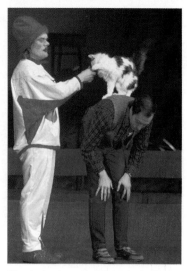

The domestic cat is without doubt the most difficult feline to train for the circus.

Top billing for the cat

The first cat devised for the silver screen was Felix the Cat. This cat was created in 1919 in the United States and quickly became one of the most famous animals in the world, enjoying one success after another during the inter-war years. The hero of hundreds of episodes, this resourceful, intelligent tomcat was also something of a poet, despite his great love of roast chicken. Felix

This brightly coloured German engraving dating from the end of the 19th century depicts a feline circus straight out of the artist's imagination.

Feline competitions which bring together breeders and cat lovers are major events where successfully elected champions can ensure a highly envied pedigree for their descendants. The first competition took place in July 1871 when 160 cats were shown to the public at Crystal Palace. But only in 1887 pedigrees were registered systematically. Since 1895 the most prestigious feline competitions in the USA take place at Madison Square Garden.

subsequently became a comic strip character in England, enjoying as much popularity as at the cinema, only to be outwitted by a common mouse called Mickey. In 1939, a new feline star called Tom was born, produced by Metro-Goldwyn-Mayer and drawn by William Hanna and Joseph Barbera. Although as likeable as Felix, Tom is an unhappy hero, because his stage partner Jerry, a little grey mouse, 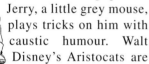 plays tricks on him with caustic humour. Walt Disney's Aristocats are

The confrontation between Tom and Jerry is endless. The mouse always fools the cat.

Essentially friendly by nature, Felix, the father of all comic strip cats, is capable of forging bonds of friendship even with mischievous mice.

The relationship between Sylvester and Tweety Pie is a perfect example of schizophrenia. Natural enemies, the two accomplices become allies when in a tricky situation.

Sylvester and Tweety Pie form one of the most enduring couples in America.

unquestionably the greatest feline stars. In this classic of the American cinema, the common alley cat falls in love with a delightful high society cat. He woos the enchantress with his courage, intelligence, and humour, and the popularity of their adventures with the public has not diminished in over thirty years.

Fritz, the bad cat

This character was created by the American artist Robert Crumb at the end of the 1960s,

Rich, beautiful, and refined, the heroine of *The Aristocats* is a seductress.

but became more famous during the 1970s. Fritz has been defined as the antithesis of Felix the Cat. This New York hoodlum is completely debauched, a rebel who fears neither God nor man, with a liking for wild women and seedy dives. Fritz ends up being assassinated in the last episode. In revolt against the established moral order, Fritz the Cat is the fruit of a period which questioned an entire social order and the taboos which it entailed.

With Fritz the Cat, the nice guy heroes are put out to grass. Fritz is an adult character who enjoys a life of sex, drugs and rock 'n' roll.

A monumental Walt Disney production, *The Aristocats* is not so much a cartoon as a spectacular in which each cat, even if a mere alley cat, is a star in its own right.

The Cat as Salesperson

A Hollywood actor, sometimes even acknowledged by the Patsy Awards for Best Animal Actor, the cat has also made its mark in the field of advertising. Its acting talents are not just limited to cat food; its sensual image combined with its unbridled taste for comfort are used in a variety of settings. A cat may suggest the gentle purring of a car's motor, or it can add prestige to a make of computers, a brand of cigarettes, chocolate, or washing powder – or even cheese!

An alley cat, hero of *The Aristocats*, symbolizing the American Dream.

CATS
around the world

North America

Atlantic Ocean

*Pumas, jaguarondis and ocelots are the closest relatives of the cat, who live in Central America.

South America

Pacific Ocean

Arctic

*The European lynx and the European wild cat are the only members of the cat family living in Europe.

Asia

*The caracal lynx, the fishing cat and their close relatives are small felines who can be found in the whole of Asia.

Europe

Africa

The African wild cat *felis lybica* and the serval are much less known cats than the leopard or the lion.

Indian Ocean

Australia

long-haired cats

short-haired cats

wild cats

Antarctic

CATS

Principal Species

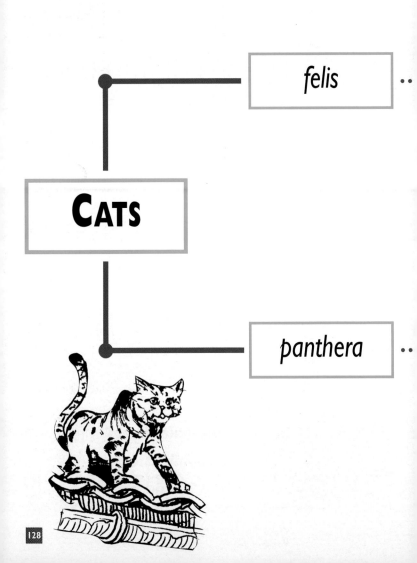

felis ..

CATS

panthera ..

The jaguarondi haunts American tropical forests. With his plain coat and his short legs he resembles a mongoose.

The serval is a small cat living in the African bush. He survives on birds and small mammals.

The European wild cat is a very discreet animal. A disturbed wild cat can be very aggressive.

The long-haired persian cat and the short-haired Siamese cat together are at the origin of most purebred domestic cats.

The tiger is the largest living cat. He can reach a length of more than three meters and weigh 200 kg.

The lion, who is widely held to be the king of the animals, is the only cat who knows how to roar.

Creative workshop

*Having studied all of these creatures,
it's time to get creative.*

*All you need are a few odds and ends and a
little ingenuity, and you can incorporate
some of the animals we've seen into
beautiful craft objects.*

*These simple projects will give you further
insight into the animal kingdom presented in
the pages of this book.*

*An original and simple way to enjoy
the wonderful images of the animal kingdom.*

Cat candle-holder

*W*ith *its whiskers bristling and its tail standing on end, this metal cat is trying to look fierce – but all it will do with its gentle light is mount guard over your evenings.*

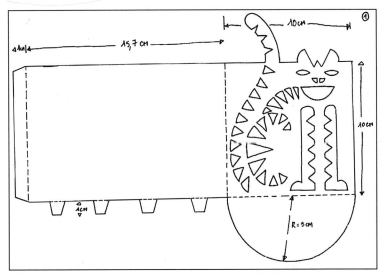

Photocopy the design and blow it up to the desired size.

Cutting the metal

• Place the photocopy on the sheet of pewter, stick it down at the four corners with the adhesive tape and place the sheet on top of the wooden board.

• Cut out the design with the cutter, cutting

through the sheet of paper and the sheet of pewter at the same time. Go over each line several times with the cutter blade to make sure it cuts right through the metal.

Making the grooves

• Only go over the dotted lines (which will be folded) with the cutter blade once, so as to score a groove into the thickness of

small tabs for the base; then close the candle-holder making sure that the back is bent into a curved shape matching the curved edge of the base.

• Glue the underside of the little tabs onto the base and glue the vertical tab to the front.

The whiskers

• Cut the wire into four pieces and

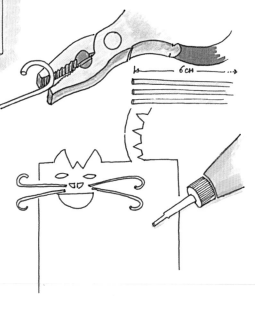

use the pliers to twist one end of each piece into a curl.

• Stick the pieces of wire either side of the nose, using a little glue on the tip of each piece.

the metal without actually cutting it. Press the shape of the candle-holder out of the sheet and fold along the scored lines with the help of a ruler placed along the line of each fold.

Folding

• Bend the back into a curve and fold the long vertical tab for gluing and the four

Finishing

• Finally, cut a piece of plastic the same size as the front of the candle-holder and slip it inside just behind the front, using a drop of glue or a small piece of adhesive tape to stick it in place. Place a flat candle (of the type sold in a small metal dish) inside the candle-holder.

Materials

• A sheet of pewter for cutting, at least 30 x 20 cm • A cutter • Super-glue
• Adhesive tape • A pair of pliers for bending and cutting • 25 cm of galvanised wire • A sheet of coloured plastic (e.g. a divider from a loose-leaf file, an exercise book cover etc.)

Cat silhouette

*T*his mischievous cat has come down from the city rooftops to play on your wall. Use flexible wire to make it.

Making the cat

• Blow up the drawing to A4 size.
• The cat is made up of two lengths of wire which you bend into the shape of the drawing: one piece for the head, tail and back paw and the other for the two front paws.
• Use a third little piece to fasten these two pieces together.

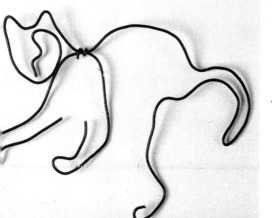

• This material can be used to create any silhouette of your choice.

Material

• About 1.50 m of wire sheathed in black plastic, available from the D.I.Y. section of the big department stores

Cat book-mark

*A*nd why not blue? With its tail curled around it, this hieratical cat will mount guard faithfully over whatever you are reading.

To make the cat

• Photocopy the design and blow it up to the desired size. Copy the enlarged design onto the tracing paper.

• Cut the sheet of Bristol board in two and stick the two pieces together with the glue spray.

• Go over the reverse side of the pattern with the drawing pencil. Place the sheet of tracing paper on the double thickness of Bristol board and stick the four corners down with adhesive tape. Make a transfer of the part to be painted (shown in blue on the pattern). Remove the tracing paper and stick a piece of the transparent adhesive film on top of the drawing, after first having stuck your hands to the sticky side several times so as to make it slightly less sticky.

• Cut through the thickness of the film with the cutter, pressing very lightly so as not to cut the Bristol board underneath. Using this stencil, paint the area you have cut away (allowing the paint to lap over onto the transparent film).

• Allow to dry and remove the transparent film carefully.

• Then stick some transparent film onto both the reverse and front sides of the Bristol board and rub it with a fine cloth so that the film sticks down well with no air-bubbles. Place the tracing on top, aligning the drawings, and hold it in place with adhesive tape at all four corners. Cut out the shape of the cat, working slowly so as to avoid the cutter slipping off its line at a tangent in the curves and without forgetting to cut out the eye.

Materials

• An A4 sheet of 250g Bristol board
(21 x 29.7 cm) • An A4 sheet of tracing paper
• A cutter • a spray-can of fixative (of the type used for mounting pictures) • Adhesive tape
• Ultramarine blue paint (acrylic or gouache)
• a medium round paintbrush • An A4 sheet of transparent matte adhesive film • A wooden board or cutting mat • A drawing pencil

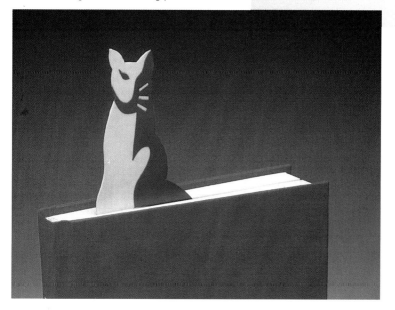

Cat carrot-cake

*T*his cake will surprise everyone, both with its unusual ingredient – carrot – and its unusual shape: a lovely great stripy pussy-cat woken up from its cat-nap.

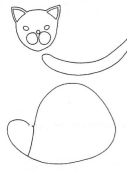

The cake

• Mix the sugar, the eggs and the fat in a large bowl .
• Mix the flour, yeast and salt in another bowl.
• Mix the contents of both bowls together.
• Add the cinnamon, the almonds, the coconut and the carrot.
• Pour the mixture into a greased cake-tin.

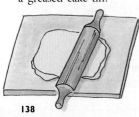

• Place in a medium oven (gas mark 3-4, i.e. approximately 180°C) for about an hour.

The cat

• Roll out the marzipan with a rolling pin.
• Cover the cake carefully with the marzipan, using the jam or marmalade to stick it to the cake. Remove any excess marzipan.
• Cut the shapes for the cat's head, paw and tail out of the remaining marzipan. Brush on egg white to hold them in place and stick them on top of the cake. Coil the cat's tail around its body.
• Mix two or three teaspoons of orange food colouring with approximately 200g of marzipan. If the mixture is too liquid, add some icing sugar.

• Roll out the marzipan with a rolling pin and cut it into strips. Stick them onto the cake with the egg white to make the cat's stripes.
• Mould the cat's paws, ears and nose out of white icing.
Use white icing to stick on the sweets for the eyes. Draw the cat's whiskers and claws with the black icing.

Ingredients

The cake
• Two cups of caster sugar • One and a half cups of oil or margarine • Four eggs
• Two cups of flour • Two teaspoons of yeast • A teaspoon of salt • Two teaspoons
of cinnamon • A cup of ground almonds • A teaspoon of vanilla essence • A cup
of grated coconut • A cup of grated carrot

The cat
• 750g of yellow marzipan • One 250g packet of
ready-to-use white icing • One tube of black icing
for writing • Two round sweets (such as aniseed
balls) or two redcurrants or two raisins for the
eyes • Two tablespoons of marmalade or jam
• One egg white • A paintbrush • Icing sugar
• Orange food colouring

Acknowledgements:

The publishers would like to thank all those who have contributed to this book,
in particular:
Guy-Claude Agboton, Antoine Caron, Jean-Jacques Carreras, Michèle Forest,
Anne Jochum, Nicolas Lemaire, Hervé Levano, Marie-Bénédicte Majoral,
Kha Luan Pham, Vincent Pompougnac, Marie-Laure Sers-Besson, Emmanuèle Zumstein

Illustration: Frantz Rey

Translation: Kate Clayton - Ros Schwartz Translations, Huw Jones

Impression: Eurolitho - Milan
Dépôt légal: September 1998
Printed in Italy